Seasons of Laughter

FOR TEACHERS

Also by Janet Colsher Teitsort

Rainbows for Teachers
Treasures for Teachers

Seasons of Laughter

FOR TEACHERS

Janet Colsher Teitsort

Baker Books

A Division of Baker Book House Co
Grand Rapids, Michigan 49516

Published by Baker Books
a division of Baker Book House Company
P.O. Box 6287, Grand Rapids, MI 49516-6287

Second printing, May 1998

Printed in the United State of America

ISBN 0-8010-1135-3

Scripture quotations identified KJV are from the King James Version of the Bible.

Scripture quotations identified NIV are from the HOLY BIBLE, NEW INTERNATIONAL
VERSION®. NIV®. Copyright © 1973, 1978, 1984 by International Bible Society. Used
by permission of Zondervan Publishing House. All rights reserved.

Scripture quotations identified TLB are from *The Living Bible,* copyright © 1971 by
Tyndale House Publishers, Wheaton, Illinois. Used by permission.

Thanks to Emily Malda, Christina Vanden Bosch, Calvin Van't Land, and Taylor
Veenstra for producing the artwork

For current information about all releases from Baker Book House, visit our web site:
http://www.bakerbooks.com/

To the
joy of the Lord
and
to my grandchildren,
Justin, Carol, Elizabeth,
Thomas, and Hannah,
who fill my life
with love and laughter

Contents

Preface

A teacher's work is sprinkled with moments of hilarity. A child says or does something unexpected, and our day is sugarcoated with granules of joy. We plan to jot down these moments of laughter just as soon as we find the time. Sometimes we remember, but other times we forget. Often we scribble accounts of funny incidents on scraps of paper that get lost in the shuffle on our desks. We need an organized system that allows us to record these moments and to keep our collection growing throughout our entire teaching career.

Seasons of Laughter for Teachers is a book for this purpose. Filled with seasonal prayer-poems and quotes, it also contains journaling pages for your funny stories. This book will provide answers to "Where do I write it?" and "Where did I put it?" Keep *Seasons of Laughter for Teachers* on your desk and watch your priceless collage of gems grow. The book is not dated by the year, so it may serve you for several years.

The Scripture references support the fact that our Savior, the Lord Jesus Christ, especially enjoyed children during his stay on earth. The picture "Jesus Laughing" (Praise, Screen Printe, Copyright 1989) has long been a favorite of mine and has inspired the writing of this book. I can imagine that if Christ were visible in the classroom, he would be enjoying a hearty laugh with the children.

To my family, friends, and The Open Door Christian Writers who have prayed and encouraged me throughout the writing of this book, may God fill your lives with his abundant joy. Special appreciation also goes to

Bev Behrman, Judy Brewer, Nancy Crabill, Cindi Franke, Jean Hickey, Dolores Honeycutt, Alice Hughes, Sarah Hunton, Janet Knight, Carol Layman, Deanna McCullough, Nita McNealy, Marcia Ogle, Candy Scaggs, Mary Ann Smith, Rob Smith, Dorothy Stephens, Christi Reynolds, Carole Rice, Sherril Tarplee, Kathy

Taylor, and Roberta Taylor for sharing some delightful gems with me.

My husband, John, for believing in me. Thanks, too, for proof-reading. Your expertise is greatly valued.

Norma Chapman and Deanna McCullough for taking time from your busy schedules to assist with the proofreading. Your keen eyes are a blessing.

The staff and students at South Decatur Elementary, who add joy to my teaching.

I couldn't have done it without you.

Like the coolness of
snow at harvest time is
a trustworthy messen-
ger to those who send
him; he refreshes the
spirit of his masters.

Proverbs 25:13 *NIV*

September

We can rejoice ... when we run into prob-
lems and trials for we know that they
are good for us—they help us learn to be
patient. And patience develops strength
of character in us and helps us trust
God more each time we use it until
finally our hope and faith are strong and
steady.

Romans 5:3-4 *TLB*

SEPTEMBER LINES

Springy feet
  Skippy feet
    Stompy feet

  Flying hands
  Flinging hands
Fingerprinting hands

Wiggly bodies
  Waggly bodies
    Waddly bodies

Waving in a line

Father, why can't
my students walk
in line?
What does the
mother duck know
that I don't know?

Bewildered, I watch
as students go up
and down the halls.
The concept of the
word *walk* seems
to have eluded them.

Many times a day
teachers voice
the words "Walk, please!"

Some days I wish we
had a recording implanted
in us. Then, like the
dolls with the pull cords,
we could reiterate the phrase
using a variety of inflections,
saving our voices
and our patience.

I realize it is only the
first month of school.
Am I overreacting,
expecting too much?
I'm only trying to
teach them order and
discipline. I know
that is important.

Father, give me patience
and techniques as I
go about this task.

Remind me to pour
out the praise when
they respectfully comply.

Who knows?
By October
I may have
my ducks in a row.

LAUGH LiNES &
JOURNALING PAGES

A student who had half-heartedly listened to the previous morning's announcements arrived carrying a small United States flag in her backpack. The teacher questioned her, "Kristen, why did you bring an American flag?"

"Well, the principal said to bring a flag."

"Oh, but he meant a flag for flag football."

Shrugging her shoulders, she sighed. "Well, how'd I know? I don't play football."

LAUGH LINES &
JOURNALING PAGES

LAUGH LINES &
JOURNALING PAGES

During the Girl Scouts' annual drive for Brownie membership, the classroom teacher was checking for returned registration sheets.

"Becky, did you bring back your sign-up sheet?"

"No," she responded. "My mommy says I can't be a cupcake."

LAUGH LiNES &
JOURNALING PAGES

During a lesson
about seasons, the
teacher said, "Tell me
about autumn."
The little boy
was puzzled for a
moment, then his
face brightened. "Oh,
you mean Autumn
and Eve."

LAUGH LINES &
JOURNALING PAGES

It was the beginning of the school year for a group of first graders. One bright boy seemed to have all the answers. The boy next to him was in a state of amazement at his new friend's knowledge.

As the class prepared to do math, a child in the back row asked, "What is two plus two?"

Without batting an eye, the scholar up front announced, "Four!"

"How'd you know that?" asked his neighboring friend. "Did you go to the high school before you came here?"

LAUGH LINES &
JOURNALING PAGES

While reading a story to her class, a primary teacher noticed a boy in the back row busily at work with his pencil. She guessed that he might be writing on his desk. "Michael, are you writing on your desk?"

"No," came the faint reply.

A short while later his pencil activity caught her eye again. "Michael, you'd better not be writing on your desk."

"I'm not," he assured her.

She continued reading. A few minutes later she saw that he had resumed his activity. "Michael," she scolded, "did you hear me? Do you want to buy that desk?"

"Why no," he answered. "I already have one at home."

October

But be transformed by the renewing
of your mind.

Romans 12:2 *NIV*

A merry heart doeth good like a
medicine.

Proverbs 17:22 *KJV*

THE METAMORPHOSIS

October—when the
colors are as sharp
as an apple is tart,
and my classroom
is ablaze with color.

Golds, greens, and
russets blend together
in my students' artwork
as effectively as our
phonetic sounds.

Change is evident
throughout.
Caterpillars,
snug in cocoons,
nestle in jars
with hole-punched lids.

But the greatest
metamorphosis is occurring
within my students.

Studiously, I labor to
see them transformed
by their growth
in knowledge.

This afternoon I
shared the story
of a caterpillar
who had eaten his fill
and had become very ill.

One of my students,
weary of illustrating
page after page
of items that the
caterpillar had consumed,
piped up,
   "Why didn't he
   just take some
   Pepto-Bismol?"

In that moment, Lord,
you gave me
a dose of humor,
something I need daily
to remind me
to lighten up.

Thank you for the
lightheartedness
of that moment.

LAUGH LINES &
JOURNALING PAGES

A little girl was sitting by a boy whose last name was Knight. It was October and the children were writing stories. When the girl brought her story to be checked, the classroom assistant saw that she had written, "One Knight . . ." The assistant quizzed her, "Why do you have Andrew's name on your paper?"

"Well, Andrew's name is Knight and I'm writing a story about Halloween night, so I thought that's how you'd spell it."

LAUGH LINES &
JOURNALING PAGES

LAUGH LINES &
JOURNALING PAGES

A group of intermediate
students delighted in teasing
their teacher about his loss
of hair. One day a picture
depicting his premature bald-
ness appeared on his desk. On
the back was scrawled "from
ANONE MOUSE"!

LAUGH LINES &
JOURNALING PAGES

The teacher had purposely
written a sentence on the
board that contained errors.
The students were to correct
and supply missing punctua-
tion. One girl raised her hand
and announced, "You need an air
comma before the s," giving a
new twist to the definition of
an apostrophe.

LAUGH LINES &
JOURNALING PAGES

A student was struggling with his printing. Daily, the teacher encouraged him to take his time and be neater. Still, his writing was unreadable. One day she called him over to sit by her so she could help him with his writing. He quickly wrote his name in almost perfect script.

Astounded, she asked, "Timothy, how can you print so neatly when you're sitting by me and do so poorly when you're at your desk?"

Without hesitation, he supplied the answer. "It's your perfume. It smells so good, I do my best, and I just write straight."

LAUGH LINES &
JOURNALING PAGES

LAUGH LINES &
JOURNALING PAGES

LAUGH LINES &
JOURNALING PAGES

A teacher shared that her little boy was very competitive. One day he was playing a game with the baby-sitter. Each time it was his turn he prayed, "Please, God, please, please, please, let me win!" Repeatedly, he lost. Finally, the baby-sitter asked, "Why do you think you're still losing?" "Oh," he said, "God doesn't play games."

November

For God hath not given us the spirit of fear; but of power, and of love, and of a sound mind.

2 Timothy 1:7 KJV

"For I know the plans I have for you," declares the LORD, "plans to prosper you and not to harm you, plans to give you hope and a future. Then you will call upon me and come and pray to me, and I will listen to you. You will seek me and find me when you seek me with all your heart."

Jeremiah 29:11–13 NIV

A BRAVE STEP

Father, for days
this child
told me that he
didn't want to go
on our field trip
to the state park.

Baffled,
I wondered why.
Today
I found out.

This morning
he came to me.
Bravely, he told
me that he had
decided to go.
He leaned
close to me and quietly
whispered,
    "But do they
    have any bears?"

Concealing my
amusement, I
assured him that
there aren't any
bears in our locality.

Now I understand.
Fear had immobilized

him and almost caused
him to miss the
field trip. But his
courageous spirit won out.

As he returned to his seat,
I chuckled inwardly.
But I couldn't help thinking
that we adults
are just like him.

We allow our fears
to paralyze us.
Unlike him,
we don't always have
a brave spirit.

Years pass
and we don't advance
in our relationships
or careers.

Father, is it because
we're afraid of the
"bears" in our lives?

Grant us courage
that we, like this child,
may forge ahead and
experience your plan
on this field trip of life.

LAUGH LiNES &
JOURNALiNG PAGES

On the way to the gym a little girl asked her teacher, "Are there any more turkey bites?"

For a moment the teacher was stumped as she tried to figure out what the child was referring to. Then she remembered that physical education classes had been canceled the week before because an exterminator had to check the gym for termites.

LAUGH LINES &
JOURNALING PAGES

A teacher had purchased a wooden turkey for her desk. The back of it held brightly colored suckers that fanned out to make the tail. Whenever the students earned a reward, she would let them select one.

One day she heard a boy tell another, "You'd better behave or you won't get to pluck the turkey."

Sometimes peer pressure can be a blessing!

LAUGH LINES &
JOURNALING PAGES

School had been dismissed for several days due to a heavy winter snowstorm. When the students returned to class, their teacher asked if they had been snowbound.

"No," replied one little girl, "we had a blow-dryer and we just blew that snow away."

LAUGH LINES &
JOURNALING PAGES

Two little girls were overheard trying to decode a sign in the rest room. Laboriously, they struggled and finally came up with "Please flush the to-a-let."

LAUGH LINES &
JOURNALING PAGES

A small boy enthusias-
tically bounded up to the
recess teacher and
announced, "I'm playing
basketball with myself
and the score is eight to
nothin'!" Happily, he ran
back over to the court and
continued his game.

LAUGH LINES &
JOURNALING PAGES

LAUGH LINES &
JOURNALING PAGES

LAUGH LINES &
JOURNALING PAGES

A kindergarten teacher
sported a new hairdo, complete
with frosting. Her students
were surprised and a little
apprehensive to see their
brunette teacher as a blond.
That evening one of her
students told his mother,
"Mrs. Williams sure looked
different today."
"How was that?"
asked his mom.
"She had her hair, oh, what's
the word? You know,
she had her hair iced."

WINTER

"As long as the earth
   endures,
seedtime and harvest,
cold and heat,
summer and winter,
day and night
will never cease."

Genesis 8:22 NIV

December

And she brought forth her
firstborn son, and wrapped him
in swaddling clothes, and laid him
in a manger; because there was
no room for them in the inn.

Luke 2:7 KJV

CHRISTMAS CUSTOMS

Father, today I taught
Christmas customs
from around the world,
and it was fitting that
I shared the story
of the nativity.

I explained that
Mary and Joseph
had to go to Bethlehem
to pay their taxes.

I told them that
Mary was expecting
a baby and needed
a place to rest, but
the city was crowded
and they couldn't
find a place to stay—
    there was no room
    in the inn.

As they sat captivated,
I longed to make
the story come
alive for them.

I described the inn
as being similar to
a modern day motel
that they might have

stayed in while
on vacation.

Then I posed the
pertinent question
    "What do you suppose
    they had out back?"
I assumed that someone
would mention the stable.
    What was I thinking?

Hands began to wave.
Searchingly, I scanned
their faces and
spotted my cherub.
This was the one.
She knew.
Her face was aglow
with knowledge.

Calling on her, I had
to suppress a giggle
when she excitedly
exclaimed,
    "A swimming pool!"

Humorous, yes,
but a sad commentary
on life in America.
    Many have never heard.

LAUGH LINES & JOURNALING PAGES

One morning a little girl walked into the classroom and announced, "I'm gonna be in big trouble if my dad doesn't get the glue before my mom gets home."

"My goodness, what happened?" asked her teacher.

"I was watching out the window for the bus when I knocked the manger scene off the VCR. It broke, but I saved the mom, dad, and God."

LAUGH LINES &
JOURNALING PAGES

LAUGH LINES &
JOURNALING PAGES

One December it became apparent that the signs of the time are seeping into a child's make-believe world of Santa and casting shadows of insecurity upon this age-old fantasy. Students had gathered around their teacher for sharing time. One little girl excitedly told the class that she had called the North Pole.

"Who did you talk to?" the teacher asked.

"Mrs. Claus."

"Wasn't Santa there?"

"No," she replied.

Looking puzzled, one of the boys asked, "Are they divorced?"

LAUGH LiNES &
JOURNALiNG PAGES

LAUGH LINES &
JOURNALING PAGES

The preschool class had just fin-
ished singing "Mary Had a Little
Lamb" when a boy told his teacher,
"The baby can play with the lamb."

Puzzled, the teacher wondered what
he was talking about. A short while
later she had to smile as it came to
her. At Christmas they had sung
"Mary Had a Baby." Now they were
singing "Mary Had a Little Lamb." No
wonder the child was confused. He
thought the two Marys were one and
the same.

LAUGH LINES &
JOURNALING PAGES

LAUGH LINES &
JOURNALING PAGES

LAUGH LINES &
JOURNALING PAGES

The reading group was in progress when the teacher became chilled. She got up quietly and went to her closet for a sweater. Returning to her seat, she draped it around her shoulders. One of the students looked at her and asked, "Why are you sittin' there with that sweater on you like a grandma?"

January

Joy fills hearts that are planning for good!

Proverbs 12:20 *TLB*

THE SNOW MAKERS

Snow is falling, but
it's not from the heavens,
nor is it spiraling downward,
drifting softly to the earth.

Instead, it's being
hurled horizontally
across the room by
the two snow makers
seated in the back.

Each afternoon our
floor is drifted with
the day's accumulation
of paper wads.

Even the fact
that they have
to shovel it clean
before dismissal,
picking up each
individual flake,
does not deter them.

I've tried reasoning,
    I've taken recess,
        and I've even
            called in the reserves,

strategically aligning
with parents to stop
the assaults.

The troops are halted
and a cease-fire proclaimed
        until
short-term memory dims
and the wads
become airborne again
producing the worst
blizzard of the year.

Is it in the genes
of all sixth-grade boys
to attempt to blanket
the classroom in white,
or is it a rite of passage?

Whatever the reason,
I will persevere
in my attempts
to control the
classroom weather.

But in the meantime,
Father, help me keep
my sense of humor.

LAUGH LINES &
JOURNALING PAGES

A boy had been absent from school with an illness. On his first day back, he came bouncing into the classroom and proudly announced, "I'm taking two bionics for my sickness!"

LAUGH LINES &
JOURNALING PAGES

One day a student approached his teacher with his hands clasped on his stomach. He was doubled over with pain. Concerned, she asked, "Tyler, what's the matter?" Greatly distressed, he groaned, "I have a crank in my stomach!"

LAUGH LINES &
JOURNALING PAGES

The small boy had been absent with an intestinal virus. Returning to school, he gave his teacher his written excuse.

Later the same day the teacher was introducing the dictionary and explaining its usage. The boy raised his hand excitedly and explained that he knew all about the dictionary. "This morning, when my mom wrote that note, she wanted to know how to spell diarrhea. She told me to go get the dictionary. Sure enough, it was in there. They have the strangest words in there."

LAUGH LINES &
JOURNALING PAGES

During indoor recess, a
first grader asked his teacher
if he could have a penny to play
a game. She handed him the
coin. Turning to his friend, he
asked, "Heads or hotels?"

LAUGH LINES &
JOURNALING PAGES

Two students were overheard discussing a queasy stomach. The first one, gesturing by flipping his hand back and forth, said, "My stomach feels off and on."

The other questioned in a surprised tone, "Your stomach feels off and on?"

The first one nodded. The second continued knowingly, "Well, that's gas."

Startled by the diagnosis, the first student asked, "What kind of gas?"

"I don't know," replied the second, "but it's gas."

LAUGH LINES &
JOURNALING PAGES

February

And the vessel that he made of
clay was marred in the hand of
the potter: so he made it again
another vessel, as seemed good
to the potter to make it.

Jeremiah 18:4 KJV

CRACKS

An assistant
was listening to
a little guy read
when she noticed he was
watching her intently.

After a short while
he questioned,
"Do you feel okay?"

"Why, of course,"
she replied.

Minutes passed
and his gaze
became a stare.
Shyly he asked,
"Do I have any quacks
around my eyes?"

"No, I don't see
anything wrong
with your eyes," she
assured him.

Shortly he spoke again,
patting her arm affectionately.
"Are you sure you're okay?
You have lots of quacks
around your eyes."

Chuckling,
she hugged him,
reassuring him
that she was okay.

Father, I keep thinking
of the spiritual parallel.

Are others able to
see the cracks in the
eyes of our souls?

Are they as compassionate
as the little boy?
Do they ask,
    "Are you all right?"
Or are they condemning?

Are we allowing the
cracks in our souls
to ruin our witness?

Father,
you are the potter
and we are the clay.
Help us to
yield willingly
as you smooth out
the cracks
in our lives.

LAUGH LINES &
JOURNALING PAGES

A primary class was discussing Abraham Lincoln when one little boy raised his hand and announced, "I know Lincoln's last name. It's Memorial."

LAUGH LINES &
JOURNALING PAGES

An elementary school held an assembly in honor of Abraham Lincoln. Prior to the program, the presenter, a direct descendant of America's sixteenth president and a look-alike in his Lincoln attire, was walking down the hall. At the same time, a teacher sent a little girl to the office on an errand. Returning, she quipped, "I just saw a dollar bill guy out there!"

LAUGH LINES &
JOURNALING PAGES

A teacher stopped by a
neighboring classroom. She
complimented the students
on the silhouettes they had
made of George Washington
and Abraham Lincoln. One
little boy proudly told her,
"Yep, we've been learnin' all
about that ham guy."

LAUGH LINES &
JOURNALING PAGES

_____

_____

_____

_____

_____

_____

_____

_____

_____

_____

_____

*A class of first graders
had been studying George
Washington and Abraham
Lincoln. Checking to see
what they knew about cur-
rent events, the teacher
asked, "Who is the
president of the
United States today?"
A little girl, with her
hand waving wildly, declared,
"George Clinton!"*

LAUGH LINES & JOURNALING PAGES

A teacher overheard one student informing another, "If you're Catholic, you get cathlatized, and if you're Baptist, you get baplatized."

"But Kevin," the teacher interjected, "I'm Catholic and I've been baptized."

Looking at her with a puzzled expression, he asked, "Well, are your parents alike or different?"

LAUGH LINES &
JOURNALING PAGES

SPRING

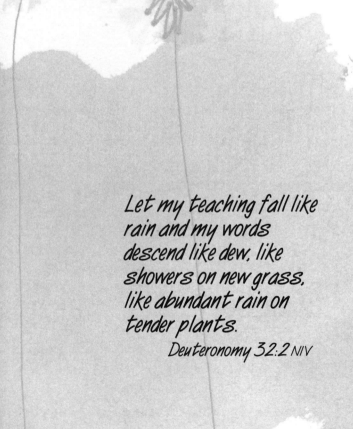

Let my teaching fall like rain and my words descend like dew, like showers on new grass, like abundant rain on tender plants.

Deuteronomy 32:2 *NIV*

March

All the earth shall worship you and
sing of your glories.

Psalm 66:4 *TLB*

SPRING VIBRATIONS

Lacy clouds,
like decorative pillows,
are tossed about on
God's sky-blue spread.

Sprigs of green
mingle with winter's
tow-colored carpet
like variegated yarn.

Scents twirl in the breeze,
entwining the fragrances
of honeysuckle
and wild onions,
wrapping them
around us like curling ribbon.

Metal abrades metal
as squeaky swings screech,
begging for their
spring anointing of oil.

Children's voices
ride the gentle wind,
seesawing with
an excited cadence.

All is well until our
spring day is shattered
by thunderous vibrations
from overhead.

Seconds pass
and silence returns,
shocking us with
its counterpoint.

Stunned
faces turn upward
and eyes search
the heavens
for the noisy offender.
Only a streak of puffiness
that looks like a soda straw
stretches among the clouds.

The stillness is
splintered with laughter
as one small observer
speaks with conviction,
    "Now, that's what I
    call a G. I. Joe plane!"

LAUGH LINES &
JOURNALING PAGES

A student told his teacher that he was learning to play the piano.

"That's great! What songs are you working on?" she asked.

"So far," he told her, "I've learned to play 'When the Saints Go Marching Down' and 'Yankee Doodle Downdey.'"

LAUGH LINES &
JOURNALING PAGES

LAUGH LINES &
JOURNALING PAGES

A mother was going to bring cupcakes for her child's birthday. Before the designated time of arrival, the teacher reminded the children to be polite.

One boy raised his hand and said, "Yes, we have to treat her with respect."

LAUGH LINES &
JOURNALING PAGES

LAUGH LINES &
JOURNALING PAGES

LAUGH LINES &
JOURNALING PAGES

An expectant teacher was giving an English lesson on singular and plural nouns. In an attempt to clarify the usage, she commented, "Each person in this school would be singular." A student in the back row raised his hand promptly and blurted out, "Except you. You're plural."

LAUGH LINES &
JOURNALING PAGES

One spring, a kinder-
gartner arrived home with
her pockets overflowing
with playground gravel.
"Lindsay," her mother
asked, "why do you have
all these rocks in your
pockets?"

"Well, the cafeteria
lady said that if I was
going outside I'd better
put some rocks in my
pockets or I'd blow away."

LAUGH LINES &
JOURNALING PAGES

April

The wisdom of the prudent is to give thought to their ways.

Proverbs 14:8 *NIV*

A MODERN PROVERB

Like wildflowers
springing up,
garage sales
dot America's lawns
with variety and color.

Moms and Dads
throw open the closets and
raise up the garage doors,
revealing
Junior's and Junette's
outgrown clothing and toys.

Basements are scoured
for profitable whatnots
and castoff appliances.

One little girl
arrives at school
wearing a
new-to-her outfit that
bears the logo
of a state university.

Thrilled, she models
her new fashion as she
proudly announces,
"Mom bought it for me
at a garage sale."

"A garage sale?"
questions one
little guy.

"Yes, a garage sale,"
she replies.

Then in a drawling
tone he speaks
with the wisdom
of Solomon,
issuing a modern proverb:
  "Well,
  garage sale stuff,
  well,
  that's the best stuff,
  'cause
  it's already been
  checked out!"

LAUGH LINES &
JOURNALING PAGES

"You look dezausted," a small tyke told his teacher.

"What makes you think so?" she asked.

"Well," he said, "your eyes are great big and your hair sticks out."

LAUGH LINES &
JOURNALING PAGES

LAUGH LINES &
JOURNALING PAGES

A little girl asked if she could bring her dog, Co-Co, to school. The teacher agreed and a time was set. The day arrived and the girl happily told her peers that her mom was bringing Co-Co after last recess.

When the children lined up to go outside to play, another child tugged on the teacher's sleeve, whispering, "I don't want any of what Sherry's mom is bringing."

Surprised, the teacher asked, "What do you think she's bringing?"

"I heard Sherry say her mom is bringing cocoa, and I don't like it!"

LAUGH LINES &
JOURNALING PAGES

During a writing assign-
ment, a boy who lived on a
farm asked his teacher, "How
do you spell Eeny, Meeny, and
Miny? I am writing a story
about my pigs."
Unable to resist, she joked,
"What happened to Moe?"
In a very serious manner, he
replied, "Oh, we couldn't
afford him."

LAUGH LiNES &
JOURNALING PAGES

A student was thrilled about becoming an uncle for the first time. When the time for the birth arrived, the boy's sister entered the hospital to have her labor induced. Aware of this fact, a teacher commented to the student, "I hear you're about to become an uncle."

Excitedly, the boy replied, "I sure am! They're going to start reducing her today."

LAUGH LINES &
JOURNALING PAGES

A Sunday school teacher was discussing miracles with a group of primary students. "Do miracles still happen today?" she asked.

After considerable buzzing in the ranks, one third grader came up with an example. "If you miss six on a test and you still get a B, that's a miracle!"

May

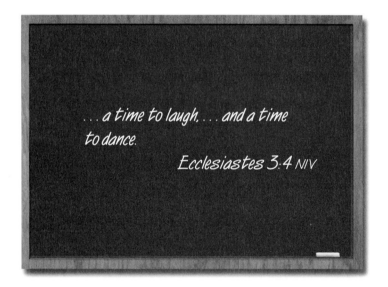

. . . a time to laugh, . . . and a time to dance.

Ecclesiastes 3:4 *NIV*

PLAY BALL

Spring breezes and warm
sunlit days compel us
to hold our P. E. class in
God's giant gymnasium
with a green grassy floor.

Attempting a rousing
game of kickball,
my first graders
flitter from base to base
like butterflies fluttering
from flower to flower.

Joy jingles in the breeze
as my students glide
on wings of freedom
like the birds soaring
overhead.

Little League professionals,
trained by summer
evenings at the ballpark,
are easily agitated
by rookie classmates
who don't understand
the concept of the game.

"It's just for fun," I tell them.
"Let's all be good sports."

A quick glance at our
makeshift diamond
gives validity
to their complaints.

"We need to pay attention!"
I say in my most
authoritative voice.

The words barely
escape my lips
when the third baseman
turns a cartwheel
and two girls
in the outfield lock hands
and spin like tops.

Like soda foam rapidly rising,
bubbles of laughter swell,
spilling over
in waves of hilarity
as the kicker's shoe catapults
in the air.
Joining in
the fun, he explains,
   "Oops! I forgot to tie it!"

The spontaneous
sidesplitting slapstick
leaves us in stitches,
bonding us with merriment.

Father, thank you
for the gift of humor.
May the cares of
this world never
be allowed to squelch
the joy
of the unexpected.

LAUGH LINES &
JOURNALING PAGES

Spring had arrived when a first grader brought in a ring-necked snake, snug in a jar. The teacher, working at her desk, overheard one boy questioning his class-mates, "Do you know why a ring-necked snake has rings?"

"No, how come?" they asked.

Feigning knowledge, he replied with seriousness and smugness, "It's because he's married."

LAUGH LINES &
JOURNALING PAGES

It was inventory time and all the teachers were scurrying around gathering the data for their forms. A teacher stopped by a neighboring classroom to get the serial number off the VCR that they shared. One student, overhearing snatches of the conversation, interjected, "Cereal? I like cereal. What kind ya got?"

LAUGH LINES &
JOURNALING PAGES

Two students were over-
heard discussing a book
report selection. The one
asked, "Where did you find a
book on that topic?"

The second student
replied, "I looked in the card
catalog."

"You're kiddin'!" the first
student responded. "You
mean people really use the
card catalog? I thought only
teachers did that."

LAUGH LINES &
JOURNALING PAGES

LAUGH LINES &
JOURNALING PAGES

A primary student
asked his teacher, "Is Mrs.
McKee going to have a
baby? She's wearing
those turtle clothes."

LAUGH LINES &
JOURNALING PAGES

Rest rooms often provide
the setting for humorous
comments by youngsters. In
an older structure that housed
an elementary school, the
teachers shared the rest
room facility with the students. One stall was
designated for faculty.
One day a little angelic face
appeared from under the students' side, peering up into the
teachers' stall. Smiling, she
said, "Why, hello, Mrs. Bee.
I thought that was you. I
recognized your shoes."

SUMMER

He maketh me to lie down in green pastures: he leadeth me beside the still waters. He restoreth my soul.

Psalm 23:2-3 KJV

June

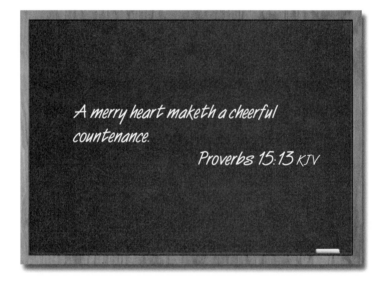

A merry heart maketh a cheerful countenance.

Proverbs 15:13 *KJV*

THE SWITCH

Father, through your
guidance I made the switch
from first to sixth grade,
and it has been fun,
  and I might add,
  enlightening.

After I adjusted to
bigger bodies and
bigger desks, I began
to glimpse the world
through the eyes
of the preadolescent.

It wasn't long before
I discovered that
preteens have their
own agenda, which they
seek to keep hidden from
the adult population.
  We must never tell them
  that we're on to them.

"I don't care" means
"I do care," and there is
a method to their madness.
They plan their work and
work their plan, and I'm
not talking about lessons.

I soon learned that
anything they tell me
must be checked out.

By day two my gullibility
had gone out the window,
almost. There was the incident
with the rattlesnake eggs.
  Now, why would I have
  believed there were really
  rattlesnake eggs
  in the envelope?

In defense, I have to add
that they had just come from
science and it was early
in the year.

What joy, what hilarity
I gave them when I reached
for the envelope,
and as it began
to shimmy and shake,
I screamed,
pitching it into the air.
  I made their day.

Who can say when the exact
moment of bonding occurs?
Is it in sorrow,
in laughter,
or in just being?
Sometime, somewhere,
during the journey
of the year,
it has happened.

Father, I'm glad I made
the switch.

LAUGH LINES &
JOURNALING PAGES

"My goodness, your buzz
haircut is growing out so
quickly," commented a teacher
to one little guy.
   "Yep, my hair grows in the
shower."

LAUGH LINES &
JOURNALING PAGES

LAUGH LINES &
JOURNALING PAGES

The cafeteria was serving a fruit drink that the kids called "the new, blue juice." The teacher asked the students how they liked it. One boy explained, "They're using us for hamsters."

"Hamsters?" she asked. "Don't you mean guinea pigs?"

"Yeah, I knew it was something like that."

LAUGH LINES &
JOURNALING PAGES

LAUGH LINES &
JOURNALING PAGES

LAUGH LINES &
JOURNALING PAGES

The kindergartners
were winding up gym
class. One little girl came
running up to her teacher
in a huff. Putting her
hands on her hips, she
fumed, "Well, I hope you're
happy! Are you happy? I
have a jean rash from all
this running!"

LAUGH LINES &
JOURNALING PAGES

While reading a story, whenever the small boy came to the word bicycle, he would say bike. The classroom assistant, wanting to be sure he recognized the difference between the two words, pointed out his error.

Nodding his head, he assured her, "I know. In the old days that's what they called it, but today it's just a bike."

LAUGH LINES &
JOURNALING PAGES

_____

_____

_____

_____

_____

_____

_____

_____

_____

A group of first graders were sharing what they wanted to be when they grew up. One boy said he wanted to be a psychologist. His teacher, while thinking that this was a wonderful choice, wondered why one so young would choose this profession. "Josh," she asked, "why do you want to be a psychologist?"

"Oh," he replied, "I just like working with bones."

Amused, she realized that he had confused psychologist with paleontologist. Relieved that he had not experienced a trauma that had pointed him toward the field of psychology, she explained the difference between the two careers.

July

You crown the year with your bounty, and your carts overflow with abundance.

Psalm 65:11 *NIV*

ENCIRCLING THE CALENDAR

It sounds like a
merry-go-round
that teachers will
never get off,
but it's a hot topic
in the field
of education.
Some schools are
even piloting it.

YEAR-ROUND SCHOOL

My first impulse
is to lament.
  *I don't want to
  give up my fun
  in the sun.
  Why, it takes me
  weeks just to
  rest and recuperate.
  How could I ever
  teach year-round?*

Father, calm my anxieties.
Help me to compute
the pluses and minuses

of offering a continual
cycle of education
for students and teachers.
  *Maybe my energies
  would not be depleted
  by spring if I had breaks
  throughout the year.*

  *Maybe students
  would be easier to teach
  if they didn't forget
  over summer break.
  Their minds would
  overflow with an
  abundance of knowledge.*

  *Maybe year-round school
  is worth a try.*

Father, keep my
heart open to change.
Give me a willingness to
try something new and
help me not to block success
with a negative attitude.

LAUGH LINES &
JOURNALING PAGES

A class was studying rocks and fossils. Several of the students brought in rocks that they had found. One little girl said, "My mom's friend brought some rocks from, (pause), oh you know, that place where God used to live."

"Do you mean Israel?" asked the teacher.

"No, that other one," she replied.

"You must mean Jerusalem," the teacher offered.

"Yes, that's it!" she exclaimed.

LAUGH LINES &
JOURNALING PAGES

July

LAUGH LINES &
JOURNALING PAGES

LAUGH LINES &
JOURNALING PAGES

One of the questions on a history test was "When and where was the Declaration of Independence signed?" The student promptly wrote her answer to the two-part question:
(1) July 4, 1776
(2) at the bottom of the page

LAUGH LINES &
JOURNALING PAGES

A student was distraught over having to move. She agonized over it for weeks. The teacher assured her that her friends would write to her and even presented the girl with a folder of stationery and self-addressed stamped envelopes. Before she moved, the girl gave the following note to her teacher: "It won't be fun wint I move. I will sin leters to you. I can wast my time doing it."

The teacher had to chuckle at the child's choice of words, for she knew that the girl had meant to say she could write when she had free time.

LAUGH LINES &
JOURNALING PAGES

LAUGH LINES &
JOURNALING PAGES

LAUGH LINES &
JOURNALING PAGES

A class was depicting words by drawing the letters and coloring them in with markers. An example would be the use of red-orange for the word hot. One student had chosen the word lazy. The teacher was surprised when the student handed it to her uncolored. "Aren't you going to color this?" she asked. "No," the student drawled, "I really don't know what color lazy is."

The teacher took a second glance at the pencil drawing, then stated, "On second thought, I think you've got it."

August

May the God of hope fill you with all
joy and peace as you trust in him,
so that you may overflow with hope
by the power of the Holy Spirit.

Romans 15:13 *NIV*

Faith by itself, if it is not accompanied
by action, is dead.

James 2:17 *NIV*

HEARTS OF HOPE

Berry brown bodies
baked by the sun
arrive wearing
fashionable school attire.

Backpacks, bearing
the logo of Disney's
summer movie,
bulge with
school supplies.

Mid-August the heat
is unbearable,
but in the classroom
we are refreshed
by the newly installed
air-conditioning unit.

Soon the memories
of bike rides, summer
camp, and the smell of
chlorine pools will fade.

Today, the scent of
newness prevails—
    new chalk,
        new crayons,
            new textbooks.

Hearts are filled with
hope and promise that
during this school year
dreams will be fulfilled,
lives will meet
with success.

One little boy
who has heard
that I am an author
smiles at me and says,
    "I know
        you can teach me
        to read 'cause you
        make books."

My heart is touched
by his faith in me.

Lord, help me not
to fail him. But motivate
him to do his part too,
for faith must be
accompanied by action.

Capsulize the hope
that is in this day and
cause it to sustain us
throughout the year.

LAUGH LINES &
JOURNALING PAGES

The first week of school is always hard for children. They have to adjust to the work load. One little girl was definitely a reluctant worker. When the classroom assistant walked by her desk, she noticed that the student hadn't put her name on her writing paper. "Suzie," she asked, "where's your name?"

Innocently, the little girl looked up and grinned. "It's still in my pencil."

LAUGH LINES &
JOURNALING PAGES

LAUGH LINES &
JOURNALING PAGES

The school year was barely under way when the teacher let a kindergartner go back to the room to get his library book. Realizing she had left a book on her desk that she needed to return, she decided to have him bring it too. When enough time had elapsed for the boy to have arrived at the room, she called over the intercom, "Jonathan, answer me," but only silence greeted her.

Again, she pushed the intercom button. "Jonathan, please answer me." Still, she was met with silence.

The third time she spoke more firmly, "Jonathan, I know you are there. Answer me, now!"

Then came the faint, quavery voice, "Hello, God."

LAUGH LINES &
JOURNALING PAGES

LAUGH LINES &
JOURNALING PAGES

A student arrived with his hair cut in a flat top. The teacher complimented him on his new style. Beaming, he told her, "Me and my dad, we both got a new blacktop."

LAUGH LINES &
JOURNALING PAGES

A teacher had won an award, and the principal had hung her picture on a designated wall of honor. The only pictures that had been placed there prior to hers were of people who had retired. A few days later a student walking by noticed the new picture and asked, "Is that teacher required?"

LAUGH LINES &
JOURNALING PAGES

A group of first graders were gathered around the breakfast menu posted on the bulletin board. "What's for breakfast?" asked one.

"It's coffee cake," answered another.

"Well, I'd better not eat. I'm not allowed to have coffee."

LAUGH LINES &
JOURNALING PAGES

Janet Colsher Teitsort is an author and elementary school teacher. She formerly taught first graders at South Decatur Elementary near Westport, Indiana, and now teaches language arts to sixth graders. Her other books include *Rainbows for Teachers* and *Treasures for Teachers* (both with Baker Book House) and *Quiet Times: Meditations for Today's Busy Woman.*